G000017128

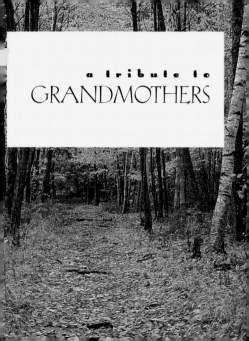

a tribute to

GRANDMOTHERS

a tribute to

GRANDMOTHERS

photographs by
catherine gehm

ARIEL BOOKS

**Andrews McMeel
Publishing**

Kansas City

www.andrewsmcmeel.com

Photographs copyright © by Catherine Gehm

Book design and production by Mspace, Katonah, New York

ISBN: 0-8362-6799-0

Library of Congress Catalog Card Number: 98-84250

CONTENTS

INTRODUCTION

The word grandmother brings to mind security, wisdom, strength, and above all, love. A grandmother is both friend and teacher, always ready with her support and guidance.

Many grandmothers no longer fit the stereotype of a gray-haired woman knitting by the fireplace.

From the career woman to the student to the homemaker, the grandmother of today is as likely to ride a bike as bake a loaf of bread. She may wear a flowered hat or a pair of blue jeans; she may tend her garden or tend her corporation; she may stay at home or travel all over the world.

What remains constant is the role our grandmothers fill. When we're small, they give us hugs and read us stories. When we're older, they offer advice when we need it and comfort when the world is getting us down. Their love is unconditional; we flourish in its light.

A
GRANDMOTHER'S
JOY

Surely, two of the most satisfying experiences in life must be those of being a grandchild or a grandparent.

—donald a. norberg

What feeling is so nice as a child's hand in yours? So small, so soft and warm, like a kitten huddling in the shelter of your clasp.

—marjorie holmes

By the time the youngest children have learned to keep the house tidy, the oldest grand-children are on hand to tear it to pieces.

—christopher morley

Why do grandparents and grandchildren get along so well? They have the same enemy—the mother.

—claudette colbert

I anticipate with much pleasure sitting on a little pink cloud in the hereafter and watching my granddaughter upsetting all her mother's most cherished convictions.

—mrs. clipston sturgis

When grandparents enter the door, discipline flies out the window.

—ogden nash

Never have children, only grandchildren.

—gore vidal

Just about the time a woman thinks her work is done, she becomes a grandmother.

—anonymous

There is a delight, a comfort, an easing of the burden, a renewal of joy in my own life, to feel the stream of life of which I am part going on like this.

—betty friedan

Perfect love sometimes does not come until the first grandchild.

—welsh proverb

I suddenly realized that through no act of my own I had become biologically related to a new human being.

—margaret mead

Becoming a grandparent is a second chance. For you have a chance to put to use all the things you learned the first time around and may have made mistakes on. It's all love and no discipline. There's no thorn in this rose.

—joyce brothers

It begins when the first baby is expected, and you think you are all in all necessary to the occasion only to find out that you are neither wanted nor expected; and then receive a hurry call at the last minute to say that after all you had better come.

—mrs. clipston sturgis

A
GRANDMOTHER
IS . . .

A mother becomes a true grandmother the day she stops noticing the terrible things her children do because she is so enchanted with the wonderful things her grandchildren do.

—lois wyse

Grandparents have a toleration
for and patience with the boys
and girls that parents lack.

—margaret e. sangster

We can go into a quiet retire-
ment, which is the traditional
stereotype of a sixty-five-year-
old, or we can take a risk and
put ourselves out where the
action is.

—salenig st. marie

Your sons weren't made to like
you. That's what grandchildren
are for.

—jane smiley

Traditionally the image of the grandmother has been one of a benign little old lady delightedly serving roast turkey and pumpkin pie to a large family. It has now become common to speak of glamorous grandmothers. As, indeed, many of them . . . are.

—jessie bernard

The trouble with looking back is that we can't change the past. We can, hopefully, talk honestly and openly with our adult children, and even make amends—but the place where we really have a second chance is with our grandchildren.

—eda leshan

Her grandmother, as she gets older, is not fading but rather becoming more concentrated.

—paulette bates alden

I loved their home. Everything smelled older, worn but safe; the food aroma had baked itself into the furniture.

—susan strasberg

Grandma was a kind of first-aid station, or a Red Cross nurse, who took up where the battle ended, accepting us and our little sobbing sins, gathering the whole of us into her lap, restoring us to health and confidence by her amazing faith in life and in a mortal's strength to meet it.

—lillian smith

It is as grandmothers that our mothers come into the fullness of their grace.

—christopher morley

EXPERIENCE
AND WISDOM

The art of being wise is the art of knowing what to overlook.

—william james

By the time we hit fifty, we have
learned our hardest lesson. We
have found out that only a few
things are really important. We
have learned to take life seri-
ously, but never ourselves.

—marie dressler

We don't receive wisdom; we must discover it for ourselves after a journey that no one can take for us or spare us.

—marcel proust

The purpose of discipline is self-discipline, and its best source is the full-time hovering presence of a grandmother. Grandmothers don't spoil children; tired parents do.

—florence king

It doesn't happen all at once.
You become. It takes a long
time.

—margery williams

Children may close their ears to
advice, but open their eyes to
example.

—anonymous

If you have knowledge, let
others light their candles at it.

—margaret fuller

When you cease to make a
contribution, you begin to die.

—eleanor roosevelt

There are two ways of spreading light—to be the candle or the mirror that reflects it.

—edith wharton

One of the signs of passing youth is the birth of a sense of fellowship with other human beings as we take our place among them.

—virginia woolf

Grandmotherhood does not give us the right to speak without thinking, but only the right to think without speaking.

—lois wyse

Time and trouble will tame an advanced young woman, but an advanced old woman is uncontrollable by any earthly force.

—dorothy l. sayers

With every deed you are sowing a seed, though the harvest you may not see.

—ella wheeler wilcox

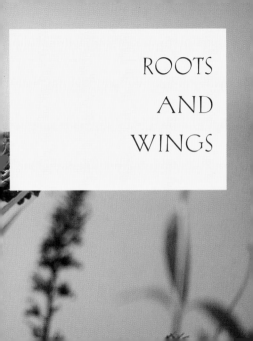

ROOTS

AND

WINGS

To be rooted is perhaps the most important and least recognized need of the human soul.

—simone weil

When you look at your life, the greatest happinesses are family happinesses.

—joyce brothers

I know why families were created, with all their imperfections. They humanize you. They are made to make you forget yourself occasionally, so that the beautiful balance of life is not destroyed.

—anaïs nin

A TRIBUTE TO GRANDMOTHERS

Other things may change us,
but we start and end with the
family.

—anthony brandt

65

Call it a clan, call it a network, call it a tribe, call it a family. Whatever you call it, whoever you are, you need one.

—jane howard

You don't have to go looking for love when it's where you come from.

—*werner erhard*

The closest friends I have made all through life have been people who also grew up close to a loved and loving grandmother or grandfather.

—*margaret mead*

YOUNG IN SPIRIT

One of the many things nobody ever tells you about middle age is that it's such a nice change from being young.

—dorothy canfield fisher

We are always the same age
inside.

—gertrude stein

Old age ain't no place for
sissies.

—bette davis

What used to be old is middle-aged now, and what used to be ancient is just old.

—joyce brothers

If you rest, you rust.

—helen hayes

I shall not grow conservative with age.

—elizabeth cady stanton

The secret of staying young is to live honestly, eat slowly, and lie about your age.

—lucille ball

Age is something that doesn't matter, unless you are a cheese.

—billie burke

We grow neither better nor worse as we get old, but more like ourselves.

—may lamberton becker

One thing is certain, and I have always known it—the joys of my life have nothing to do with age.

—may sarton

A TRIBUTE TO GRANDMOTHERS

In a dream you are never eighty.

—anne sexton

The process of maturing is an art to be learned, an effort to be sustained. By the age of fifty you have made yourself what you are, and if it is good, it is better than your youth.

—marya mannes

When I am an old woman I
shall wear purple.

—jenny joseph

Surpassingly lovely, precious
days. What is there to say ex-
cept: Here they are. Sifting
through my fingers like sand.

—joyce carol oates

Before, I always lived in anticipation . . . that it was all a preparation for something else, something "greater," more "genuine." But that feeling has dropped away from me completely. I live here and now, this minute, this day, to the full, and the life is worth living.

—elly hillesum